—— THE ——
BASIC BLUEPRINT
OF
FINANCIAL
STABILITY

JAY FOLDS

Contents

JF

JAY FOLDS

MILITARY FINANCIAL COACHING

contents

ABOUT ME

Jarquarius Folds

My name is Jarquarius Folds, and I'm the founder of Jay Folds Military Financial Coaching. I am a financial coach, a veteran (Marine), and have a Bachelor's of Science in Business Administration and a minor in Finance.

I have been a financial coach for over 6 years now. I'm sponsored by Robin's Airforce Base. My passion is to empower others with the tools and resources to help them achieve financial freedom!

JF

WHAT IS JAY FOLDS MILITARY FINANCIAL COACHING?

Jay Folds Military Financial Coaching was created to help people reach their financial goals and stay on top of their finances. Created by a financial coach, I felt the need to offer services to help people overcome their financial struggles and difficulties.

Jay Folds Military Financial Coaching is now impacting many people's lives so that they are able to keep track of their expenses and live a stress-free, comfortable lifestyle.

JF

OUR VISION

What We Envision

Our vision is to assist people by identifying their specific financial needs and challenges while teaching them how to take control of their money.

Our ultimate goal is to help people achieve financial freedom with the proper support and resources through financial coaching.

JF

WHAT IS A FINANCIAL COACH?

A financial coach is a trained professiona
who will guide you in a process that is nor
judgmental and based on your goals

Financial coaches provide support
encouragement, accountability, and tool:
to help you make informed decisions

Going through a transition? Ready to make
a change? Interested in reducing stress? A
financial coach can help with all of these
and more

WHO CAN BENEFIT FROM FINANCIAL COACHING?

- Individuals/couples who want to take control of their financial
- Individuals/couples experiencing feelings of anxiety, stress, and guilt as a result of debt
- Individuals/couples who want to learn how to become debt free
- Individuals/couples who want to learn how to invest
- Single parents struggling to make ends meet
- Anyone looking for financial guidance

WHAT WE OFFER

With our One on One Coaching course, we work with individuals and couples to help you tackle any challenges you may have in running an orderly, stress-free financial household. We will guide and mentor you as you work your way through your financial plan, by:
- Creating a cash flow plan (budget)
- Design a debt reduction plan
- Establish an emergency fund
- Initiate retirement saving
- Start a college fund
- Begin charitable giving
- Develop a specific plan to meet your financial goals

JF

WHAT

IS

SAVING

AND

HOW

TO

START

Written by: Jay Folds

JAY FOLDS MILITARY FINANCIAL COACHING

TABLE OF CONTENTS

WHAT IS SAVING?

Saving is the process of collecting money so that you can use it in the future. Saving is uncommon among people, and it lets you be prepared for any financial downfall.

Saving helps you control your spending and reach your goals.

Saving can help out in the long run. It is a smart decision to make.

WHY IS SAVING IMPORTANT?

Saving is important because it helps you plan for the future. For example, saving can help you prepare for emergencies, like a government shutdown or recession.

You could also save up for future trips or vacations.

Lastly, but most importantly, saving can help you achieve financial freedom and fulfill your desire and dream. Its an amazing way to start investing for the future

WHAT DOES A SAVINGS PLAN LOOK LIKE?

A savings plan could be something like this-you take out $50 per paycheck to save for a vacation to Hawaii at the end of the year. By the time you're ready for your vacation, you would have saved $2,600 to use on your trip. Here is a visual of what this might look like:

Gather and save

Save $50 per paycheck

Keep saving until your reach $2,600

WHAT DOES A SAVINGS PLAN LOOK LIKE?

Here's another example of a savings plan. If you save $1,000 monthly, by 10 years you'll have saved $120,000. As you keep saving more each month, your yearly savings will increase as you get older until you've reached your financial dreams!

Monthly Income	10 Years	20 Years	30 Years	40 Years
$1,000	$120,000	$240,000	$360,000	$480,000
$1,500	180,000	360,000	540,000	720,000
$2,000	240,000	480,000	720,000	960,000
$2,500	300,000	600,000	900,000	1,200,000
$3,000	360,000	720,000	1,080,000	1,440,000
$3,500	420,000	840,000	1,260,000	1,680,000
$4,000	480,000	960,000	1,440,000	1,920,000
$4,500	540,000	1,080,000	1,620,000	2,160,000
$5,000	600,000	1,200,000	1,800,000	2,400,000

HOW DO I START SAVING?

Saving can be performed in many different ways.

For example, you can save by using coupons when you go to the grocery store. This will help you save a few extra dollars every time you go shopping.

You can also save by having a jar of coins and cash at home. Put your extra change in there, and you'll be saving lots in no time! Another way to save is to open up a bank account. Your money will stay in a safe spot, and you can keep track of it easily

STEP BY STEP PLAN TO SAVE

1)   Come up with and write down your savings goals. For example, you can make a goal to save $2 every day.

STEP BY STEP PLAN TO SAVE

2)   Find ways to achieve that goal. You can collect cash, use coupons, or open a bank account to help you achieve that goal.

STEP BY STEP PLAN TO SAVE

3)   Keep track of how well you're doing. Make sure you know if you're reaching your goal or not. If you save $2 every day, you'll have $61 saved each month.

STEP BY STEP PLAN TO SAVE

4)   Increase your savings. For example, if you
want to save more each week, you can make your
goal higher and save even more. For example, if
you have save $2 per day, you'll have $730 every
year. But if you want to save more than that, like
$3.57 per day, then every year you'll save up

STARTING AGE	DAILY SAVINGS	MONTHLY SAVINGS	YEARLY SAVINGS
20	$2.00	$61	$730
25	$3.57	$109	$1,304
30	$6.35	$193	$2,317
35	$11.35	$345	$4,144
40	$20.55	$625	$7,500
45	$38.02	$1,157	$13,879
50	$73.49	$2,235	$26,824
55	$156.12	$4,749	$56,984

WHAT IS DEBT AND HOW TO ELIMINATE IT

JAY FOLDS MILITARY FINANCIAL COACHING

WRITTEN BY: JAY FOLDS

CONTENTS

WHAT IS DEBT?

Debt is when you owe
money to someone or something.

Debt can happen from different things, like buying a
house, going to college, or forgetting to pay your bills on
time.

For many people, debt can pile up over time and can
sometimes be hard to get rid of. But there are always
strategies and methods to pay off your debt completely.

WHAT IS DEBT?

Debt includes...

House payments like mortgage

Money you owe to friends/family

Monthly car payments

Credit card loans

School tuition debt

WHY SHOULD I PAY OFF MY DEBT?

The importance of getting rid of your debt

The sooner you pay off your debt, the sooner you can start gaining financial freedom. Debt is like a weight that is always on your shoulders- it can be stressful and annoying. Having debt can get in the way of you achieving your goa On top of that, debt can increase very quickly as time goes by. This why it's important to make a plar to pay off your debt as soon as yo can.

There are different ways to pay of your debt, like the snowball effec and the avalanche effect.

WHAT IS THE SNOWBALL EFFECT?

The snowball effect is when you focus on paying off your smallest debt first. This method works great to tackle your easier debts and then move forward to the harder ones. Once you pay off your smallest debt, you move onto the next smallest debt to pay off.

WHAT IS THE SNOWBALL EFFECT?

For example, let's say you had 3 loans

$2,000

$5,000

$10,000

Using the snowball effect, you would first pay off your $2,000 debt as much as you could and pay only the minimum for your $5,000 debt. Keep paying off the smaller one until you have gotten rid of it completely. Once you've done this, then you can focus on paying off the bigger $5,000 loan, and then finally the $10,000 loan.

$2,000

$5,000

$10,000

The avalanche effect is different from the snowball effect because you focus on your debt with the highest interest first.

For example, if you have a loan with 6% interest and a loan with 3% interest, in the avalanche effect you would pay off the loan with 6% interest first and pay the minimum for the 3% loan. After the 6% interest loan is paid off, you would pay off the 3% loan.

WHAT IS THE AVALANCHE EFFECT?

—

JF

WHAT IS THE AVALANCHE EFFECT?

6%

2%

3%

In the avalanche effect, you should tackle the
biggest 6% loan first.

After it is paid off, tackle then next biggest
loan- the 3% one.

Finally, once the 3% loan is paid off, you can
focus on the 2% loan.

COMPARISON

SNOWBALL EFFECT

- Tackle smallest debt first
- Put all your money towards the smallest one
- Pay the minimum amount on your bigger debts
- Move to the next smallest debt
- End up debt free

AVALANCHE EFFECT

- Tackle biggest debt first
- Put all your money towards the biggest one
- Pay the minimum amount on your smaller debts
- Move to the next biggest debt
- End up debt free

HOW TO ELIMINATE DEBT?

READY TO ELIMINATE YOUR DEBT? HERE'S A STEP BY STEP PLAN:

YOU CAN USE THE SNOWBALL EFFECT OR THE AVALANCHE EFFECT

1 FIND OUT HOW MUCH DEBT YOU ARE IN

For example, you can calculate that you have $20,000 to pay off from school tuition.

3 BE CONSISTENT

Keep up with your plan and don't fall short. Make sure you pay the proper amount off each week.

2 PUT SOME MONEY TOWARDS PAYING OFF THAT DEBT

For example, you can commit to paying off $100 each week.

JAY FOLDS MILITARY FINANCIAL
COACHING

WHAT IS
BUDGETING AND
HOW TO START

Tips for financial success

JAY FOLDS

TABLE OF CONTENTS

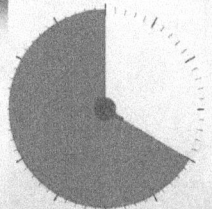

WHAT IS BUDGETING?

Budgeting is the process of creating a plan for spending your money. Budgeting is important for many reasons. For one, it helps you keep track of your expenses so that you know how you are doing financially. Another reason is that it allows you to spend the proper amount- not too much and not too little. You have just the right amount to buy what you need but not overspend. Budgeting is a great tool to help you stay on top of your finances.

BUDGET LOOK LIKE

An example of a budget could be spending $300 per week. Having this budget, you can break it down further and spend $200 on groceries, $50 on gas, and $50 on entertainment. This is a brief yet realistic example of how you can limit your spending to only what you'd like. Below is a visual outlining this weekly budget plan:

$300 → $200 Groceries

$50 Gas

$50 Entertainmer

HOW WILL BUDGETING HELP ME?

Budgeting allows you to:

- Keep track of expenses in an organized way
- Know how much you are spending every month/week
- Spend a fixed amount without overspending
- Help you map out your expenses in a visual way
- Predict how much you can save for the future
- Aid in your overall financial planning and help you achieve your financial goals

HOW DO I START?

MAKE A PLAN

This is the first and most important step for creating a budget. Write out your plans and keep them updated.

LIST OUT YOUR GOAL

Next you nee to list out yo goals, like trying to sav more or spen less money

HAVE A FIXED BUDGET

Come up with a fixed amount you're going to spend weekly or monthly. This is your limit, and you have to stay within these boudaries.

KEEP TRACK OF IT

Keeping track of you budget includes staying strictly within your limit. Don't spend too much!

ADJUST IF NEEDED

If anything changes in your finance such as increased income or le debt, adjus your budget reflect thos changes.

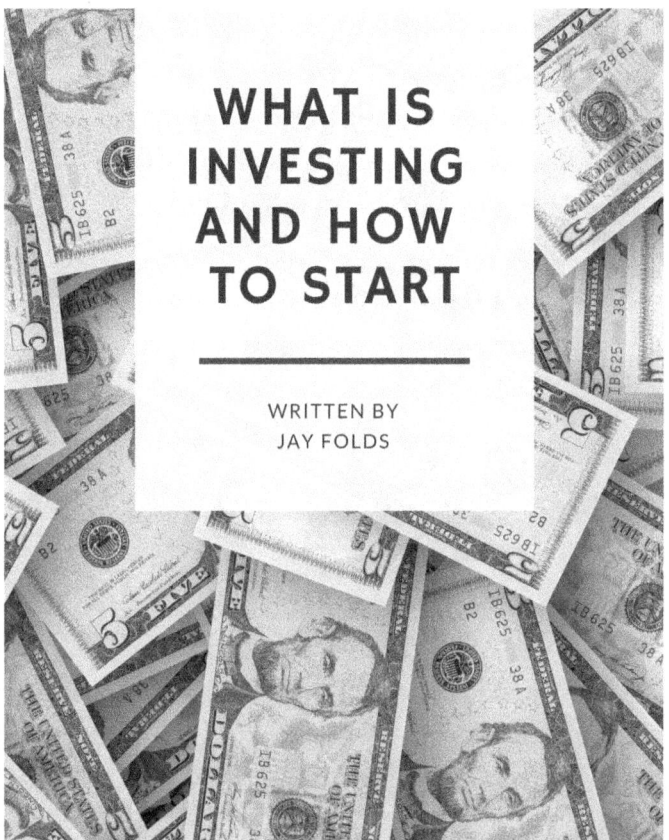

WHAT IS INVESTING AND HOW TO START

WRITTEN BY
JAY FOLDS

A guide on teaching you tips, tricks, and techniques on investing.

INVESTING | CONTENTS

JF

WHAT IS INVESTING?

Investing is when you put resources into something and hope to receive a better return. For example, you can set time and effort into building your business, and at the end have a fully functional and high-profit business.

When it comes to investing financially, it means you put money into something and expect a higher return than what you put in. The things you can put money into are the bank, stocks, or companies, and you can receive either a positive return, negative return, or flat return.

BENEFITS OF INVESTING

1

RETIRE EARLY

2

SAVE FOR
EMERGENCIES

3

PAY OFF YOUR
DEBTS

4

GIVE YOU AN ADDITIONAL
SOURCE OF INCOME

5

HAVE MONEY TO GO ON
VACATION OR MAKE
LARGE PURCHASES LIKE
CARS/HOUSES

6

EARN FINANCIAL
SUCCESS

7

BE PREPARED FOR
YOUR FUTURE

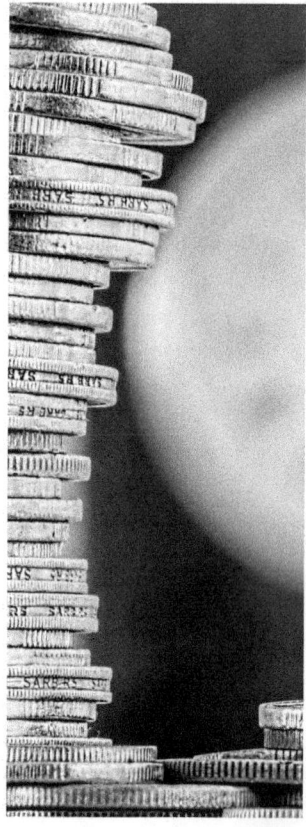

DIFFERENT WAYS
TO INVEST

There are different ways to invest
financially. You can invest by...

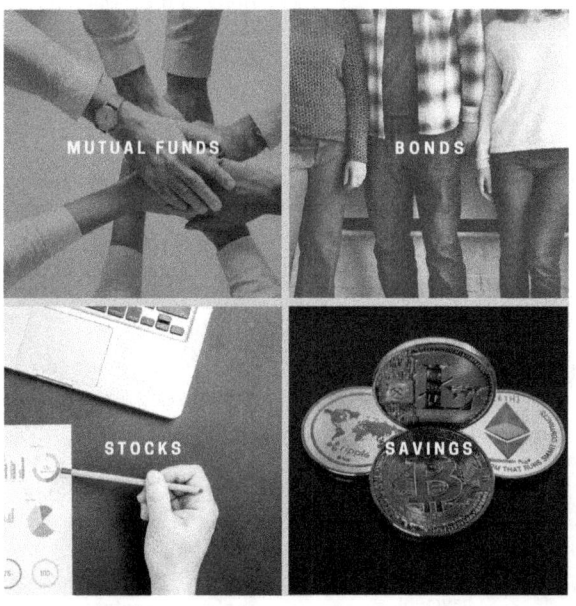

WHAT ARE MUTUAL FUNDS?

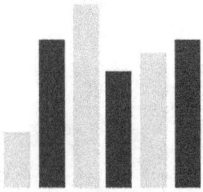

Professionals invest
your money in
different markets

Handled by experts in
the field, for a low fee
payment

A mutual fund is when you give some of your money to professionals who will invest for you on your behalf. The professionals will take your money and make different investments with it. Then, when it comes time to retrieve your money, you'll have earned a higher return without doing all the work.

Mutual funds are good because

1) the money is invested in all sorts of places and industries

2) investing is being handled by professionals

3) the fees are low

JF

WHAT ARE MUTUAL FUNDS? (EXAMPLE)

A load fund is a fund that has a fee on it. This is so that you pay the investor to do the research for you instead of doing it yourself.

Load funds are also handled by professionals.

Load Funds vs No Load Funds

If you're doing your own research and putting your own time into investing, you might want to consider no-load funds.

No load funds are funds that do not have any fees associated with them. The benefit is that they have a higher return on investment since you aren't paying fees on them.

WHAT ARE BONDS?

Bonds are a type of investment that can be seen as loans. The way bonds work is that a certain amount needed for a project or building is divided and issued to people. If someone invests in this amount, they will also receive an interest rate back every year. Then when the project is completed, the investors would earn their original money back.

This sort of investment allows people to earn money on top of their invested money. Bonds are also less risky than stocks because they are steady and schedule payments, while stocks are influenced by the market and demand.

JF

WHAT ARE BONDS?
(EXAMPLE)

For example, if the city needed to build a park that costs $10,000 in total, they could issue bonds of $1,000 to different people. To attract investors, they could offer 5% interest rates per year. Anyone who decides to purchase that bond would invest their money, while also earning $50 every year. Then, after the project is completed, they would receive the original $1,000 they put into the bond.

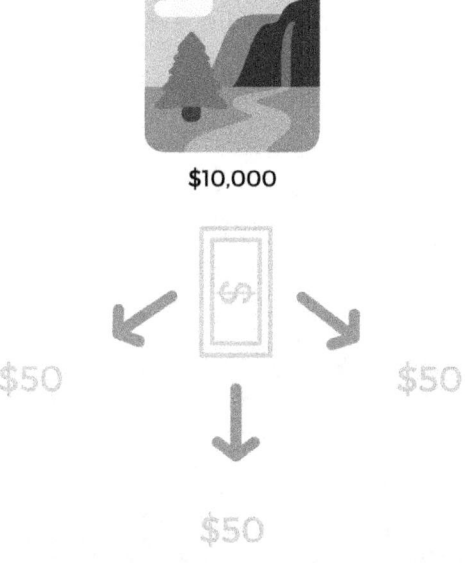

$10,000

$50 $50

$50

WHAT ARE STOCKS?

A stock is when you own a share of a company. This investing gives you a positive return when the market grows.

For example, if I gave $5,000 of my money to Google this year, and next year they increased 5%, I would earn an extra $250 that year. If I wanted to, I could sell my shares to another investor, and I would be able to cash out for $5,250. Investing wisely in stocks and making smart decisions by looking at the market growth can help you grow your income.

Here is an example of market conditions fluctuating:

WHY SHOULD I INVEST?

Investing is important for your finances because it gives you a chance to increase your wealth. Instead of having your money sit around while not being used, you can use your money towards investing and earn a higher profit. It is a wise decision to make and teaches you about how the markets work. If you invest strategically, you can expect a positive return on your money and be increasing in wealth in no time!

READY TO START INVESTING?

If you're ready to start investing, contact Jay Folds Military Financial Coaching. We'll teach you how to research thoroughly and invest appropriately, and we'll support you along the way. You'll learn tips and tricks and gain skills on how to invest for your future. Start investing today!